SPOTLIGHT
ON CHILDREN'S
AUTHORS

JUDY BLUME

WENDY MEAD

Cavendish
Square
New York

For India.

Published in 2015 by Cavendish Square Publishing, LLC
243 5th Avenue, Suite 136, New York, NY 10016

Library of Congress Cataloging-in-Publication Data
Mead, Wendy.
Judy Blume / Wendy Mead.
pages cm. — (Spotlight on children's authors)
Includes bibliographical references and index.
ISBN 978-1-62712-843-8 (hardcover) ISBN 978-1-62712-844-5 (paperback) ISBN 978-1-62712-845-2 (ebook)
1. Blume, Judy—Juvenile literature. 2. Authors, American—20th century—Biography—Juvenile literature. 3. Children's stories—Authorship—Juvenile literature. I. Title.

PS3552.L843Z775 2014
813'.54—dc23
[B]

2014001525

Editorial Director: Dean Miller
Editor: Andrew Coddington
Senior Copy Editor: Wendy A. Reynolds
Art Director: Jeffrey Talbot

Designer: Amy Greenan
Production Manager: Jennifer Ryder-Talbot
Production Editor: David McNamara
Photo Research: J8 Media

The photographs in this book are used by permission and through the courtesy of: Cover photo by David Buchan/Getty Images; LUCY NICHOLSON/REUTERS/Newscom, 4; © Jacoby/Sueddeutsche Zeitung Photo/The Image Works, 6; Carrin Ackerman for Cavendish Square, 10, 13, 22, 27, 33; Boston Globe/Getty Images, 16; © Helene Rogers/age fotostock, 20; Romain Blanquart/MCT/Newscom, 28; Los Alamos National Laboratory/TIME & LIFE Pictures/Getty Images, 30; © Henry McGee/Globe Photos/ZUMAPRESS.com, 32; LUCY NICHOLSON/REUTERS/Newscom, 34; Michael Stewart/WireImage/Getty Images, 36; Carl Lender/File:JudyBlume2009.jpg/Wikimedia Commons, 39.

Printed in the United States of America

CONTENTS

INTRODUCTION:

Telling It Like It Is

For more than four decades, writer Judy Blume has been a trusted friend for generations of readers. The experiences of her characters often mirror what's going on in her readers' lives. Suddenly, her readers realize they are not the only ones being harassed at school or whose parents are splitting up. Blume has drawn from her own life, as well as the experiences of her two children, to explore such real-life issues as sibling rivalry, body image, and bullying.

With her honest and direct style, Blume has managed to create a realistic portrait of growing up on the page. Her readers feel a special bond with her as a result. As she explained to *Newsweek*, Blume has become "a confidante to thousands of young people who write to [her] every year, in response to [her] books."

Not everyone has been so thrilled with her work. During her long career as a writer, Blume has faced numerous challenges regarding her novels. People have objected to such books as *Forever*, *Deenie*, *Tiger Eyes*, and *Are You There God? It's Me, Margaret*, claiming the subjects they covered weren't appropriate for younger readers. Many have tried to ban them from schools and libraries. According to the American Library Association, Blume is one of the most frequently challenged authors of the twenty-first century. Nevertheless, Judy Blume has followed her own personal compass regarding what she writes.

Despite the controversy that sometimes surrounds her work, Blume has enjoyed great success as an author. She has written more than twenty books, which have sold more than 75 million copies and have been translated in more than twenty-six languages.

Judy Blume graduated from
New York University in 1961, which is
near Washington Square, shown here.

Chapter 1
EARLY INSPIRATIONS

One of America's most beloved authors started out her life as **Judith Sussman**. She was born on February 12, 1938, in Elizabeth, New Jersey. She grew up as the youngest child of Rudolph and Esther Sussman. Her father was a dentist. Her mother stayed home to look after Blume and her older brother, David.

Blume told *Seventeen* magazine that her brother was quite a handful for her parents. Although he was bright, "he had such a temper that he held his breath until he turned blue" and "kicked his kindergarten teacher in the stomach on the first day of school." Compensating for her brother's behavior, Judy "tried to be perfect" to make life easier for her parents.

Born with a great imagination, Blume liked to create stories all the time. "I made up stories while I bounced a ball against the side of our house," she explained on her website. "I made up stories playing with paper dolls. And I made them up while I practiced the piano." A shy child, Blume kept these stories to herself. She never even wrote them down.

Blume was also an avid reader, and liked to visit her local library with her mother. *Madeline* by Ludwig Bemelmans was one of her favorite books. Blume also loved to watch stories projected on the big screen. After each weekly visit to the movie theater with her parents, Blume would act out what she saw. She never considered becoming a writer until she was an adult. "When I was growing up, I dreamed about becoming a cowgirl, a detective, a spy, a great actress or ballerina," Blume wrote on her website.

When Blume was in the third grade, her brother became ill. Her family decided that he needed to be in a warmer place for his health, so Blume moved to Miami Beach for two years with her brother, mother, and grandmother. Her father stayed behind in New Jersey to run his dental practice. While her father came down to Miami to visit occasionally, Blume still missed him.

Both of Blume's parents were Jewish, and she was raised in the Jewish faith. Her religion influenced some of her social life. In her town, churches and temples were centers of community life. Christians hung around mostly with other Christians, and Jews spent much of their time with other Jews. As Blume explains on her website, school was one of the places where a person's religion didn't matter.

As a teenager, Blume felt oppressed by the expectations that others had for her. "I grew up in the 1950s and I didn't like any part of it," she told *Architectural Digest*. "We were expected to be happy girls from happy families, to fit in, to be normal." For years, Blume struggled to please others and meet their expectations.

Blume's first career ambition was to be a teacher. She briefly attended Boston University, and then transferred to New York University to study education. While still in college, Blume went through a personal tragedy. Her father died shortly before she married her first husband, John Blume. The loss of her father hurt her deeply, but she had no one to confide in. "My new husband wasn't one for showing emotion or dealing with feelings," she explained in the 1999 book, *Letters of Intent.* "So I did what I knew how to do best, what I thought my father would want me to do. I pretended to be happy."

Blume graduated from college with a Bachelor's degree in education in 1961 but chose not to pursue a teaching career. Instead, like many women in the 1960s, she stayed at home to care for her children while her husband went out to work. Her daughter, Randy Lee, was born that same year. Her son Lawrence, also known as Larry, arrived in 1963. She and her family lived in New Jersey.

As an adult, Judy Blume realized that her childhood need to tell stories had never really gone away. Although she loved her family, she found she was restless and unhappy staying at home all the time, so she decided to explore her creative side. She started writing for children once her own kids were in nursery school. In 1966, she signed up for a writing class with children's author and editor Jane Lee Wyndham that was held at her old college, New York University. She actually loved the course so much she took it twice! Judy Blume would go on to use the skills she gained from the course to create books readers all over the world have loved and related to.

Published in 1969, *The One in the Middle Is the Green Kangaroo* was Judy Blume's first novel.

Chapter 2
CAREER BEGINNINGS

Judy Blume had her first taste of success with writing stories for magazines. Then, with the publication of her first children's book in 1969, *The One in the Middle Is the Green Kangaroo*, Blume officially became an author. In the book, second grader Freddy Dissel struggles with being the middle child in his family. He has to wear his big brother Mike's hand-me-downs, and put up with his annoying little sister, Ellen. A school play, however, presents Freddy with an opportunity to finally stand out from his siblings.

With her next effort, Blume focused her attention on an even bigger issue. *Iggie's House* (1970) looks at racial prejudice through the eyes of sixth grader Winnie Barringer. The book begins when Iggie, Winnie's best friend, moves away, and the Garbers, an African American family, move in. Winnie befriends the Garber kids—Glenn, Herbie, and Tina—but not everyone is so welcoming. Mrs. Landon, one of the other neighbors, doesn't like the idea of a black family living in her white neighborhood. She starts a petition to try to drive the Garbers out, and even posts a sign in their yard telling them to "go back to where they came from." Winnie can't stand Mrs. Landon, so she comes up with her own petition, and tries to gather information on other people's attitudes toward blacks.

Winnie writes about the situation in a letter to Iggie. She explains to her friend how angry she is about Mrs. Landon's treatment of the Garbers. She also tells Iggie about her frustration with Herbie Garber, who is not convinced of Winnie's intentions. He thinks that she wants to prove that she's cool by having a black friend. Many of Blume's later novels include letters, too. This writing technique allows main characters to share some of their thoughts and feelings with the reader.

The whole idea behind the novel came from Blume's own experience. "I lived in a neighborhood in suburban New Jersey that was all white," she explained in an interview on the Scholastic website. "And I liked to think about how the neighbors would handle a racially mixed neighborhood."

That same year, Blume explored another challenging topic in *Are You There God? It's Me, Margaret* (1970). Margaret Simon is trying to figure out whether she should be Jewish or Christian. Her mother is Christian and her father is Jewish, but neither parent practices their faith. They have raised Margaret without a religion. This doesn't bother her until her family moves from New York City to Farbrook, a suburb in New Jersey.

Not long after she arrives in Farbrook, Margaret finds herself being asked about her religious background. The kids at her new school seem to be either Christian or Jewish, and hang out at either the local YMCA or the Jewish Community Center. The question of

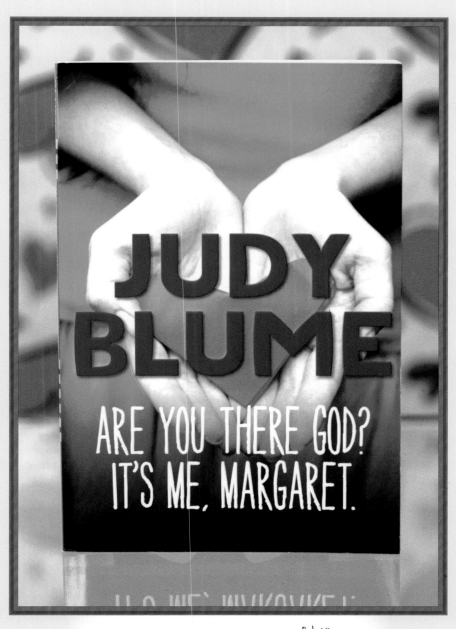

Judy Blume drew from many of her
own experiences for the novel
Are You There God?
It's Me, Margaret.

which one she should join leads her to wonder about what faith she should belong to.

Margaret decides to make religion the topic of a school project. She attends several different kinds of religious services in a temple and a couple of churches, but none of these visits have any effect on Margaret. She feels closest to God when she talks to Him while she is alone at home. Blume explained to *Tablet Magazine* that Margaret's religious experience reflects her own. "Margaret was the kind of a child I was. It was my relationship with God I wrote about." Margaret's private talks with God throughout the novel provide the reader a different perspective on Margaret as well. As Blume explained on her author page on the Random House website, "I love to get inside characters' heads, because what we think is not necessarily what we say or do."

Along with questions about religion, *Are You There God? It's Me, Margaret* also follows the emotional and physical changes that young teenage girls go through. Margaret, along with her new friends Nancy, Janie, and Gretchen, form a club called the Pre-Teen Sensations, or PTS for short. They share their interest in boys and their fascination with their own bodies, and try special exercises to increase their breast size. The PTS members are especially focused on when each of them will get her period.

While the book proved to be popular with young readers, Blume found herself under attack for some of its content. Some thought the novel painted an unfair portrait of Christianity. Others objected to Blume's honest and direct discussion of menstruation. She also

LETTERS TO JUDY

With the publication of *Are You There God? It's Me, Margaret*, Judy Blume received her first fan letter. She quickly answered—and before long, more messages from her readers followed. By the mid-1980s, Blume was receiving roughly two thousand letters a month.

Many of her fans wrote to her about their problems. Some of them seemed more comfortable writing to Blume than talking to their own parents. In an effort to help her readers, Blume put together the book, *Letters to Judy: What Your Kids Wish They Could Tell You* (1986), where she paired young people's messages and questions with her own comments. This book was intended to improve communication between kids and their parents.

had her first encounter with censorship. The principal of her own children's elementary school refused to allow the novel to be in the school's library. Still, *Are You There God? It's Me, Margaret* proved to be a groundbreaking novel, becoming one of the first books that openly addressed the physical changes young women go through.

With *Tales of a Fourth Grade Nothing*, Judy Blume became one of the most popular children's authors of the 1970s.

Chapter 3
BECOMING A BEST SELLER

With the publication of *Tales of a Fourth Grade Nothing* in 1972, Judy Blume reached new heights as a writer. The novel quickly won over young readers with its humor. The book gives readers an inside look at the challenges fourth grader Peter Hatcher faces as the older brother to Farley "Fudge" Drexel Hatcher. Blume has said that some of the inspiration for Fudge came from her own son, Lawrence.

A toddler with a talent for making trouble, there appears to be no limit to what Fudge will do. He tries to fly off the jungle gym at the park, knocking out two of his teeth. He scribbles all over Peter's school project. Fudge even gets his hands on Peter's pet turtle, Dribble, with disastrous results. All of these incidents are described in such a funny manner that the reader can't help but laugh.

Tales of a Fourth Grade Nothing has proved to be Blume's most popular book with readers. According to *Entertainment Weekly*, it has sold more than 13 million copies. In a nod to its popularity with readers, Blume decided to use one of the characters from *Tales of a Fourth Grade Nothing* for her next book. *Otherwise Known as Sheila the Great* (1972) tells the story of Peter Hatcher's archenemy,

Sheila Tubman. Sheila shares a great deal in common with Blume. As Blume writes on her website, "Sheila has all of my childhood fears—dogs, swimming, thunderstorms, night terrors." Sheila tries to hide her fears from others, usually by lying.

After the back-to-back successes of *Tales of a Fourth Grade Nothing* and *Otherwise Known as Sheila the Great,* Blume returned to the world of middle school with *Deenie* in 1973. The title character, Deenie Fenner, lives in Blume's hometown of Elizabeth, New Jersey. Her father Frank owns a gas station, and her mother Thelma has big plans for Deenie. She wants Deenie to become a model, but Deenie isn't so sure that's her dream, too. At her mother's insistence, Deenie makes trips to New York City to meet with modeling agencies. In an interview with the *St. Petersburg Times,* Judy Blume stated that the mother-daughter relationship is the main focus of the book: "[*Deenie*] is about parental expectations. It's a book about if a parent pigeonholes you—this is who you are and who I want you to be."

A health problem, however, puts Deenie's potential modeling career on hold. Deenie's gym teacher notices that something is off about Deenie's posture when she tries out for the cheerleading squad. Deenie's parents take her to several doctors who determine that she has scoliosis, a condition in which the spine develops incorrectly, growing curved instead of straight. To fix this issue, Deenie must wear a special brace.

At first, Deenie is upset about wearing the brace. She lashes out at herself, cutting her long hair off. Once used to people seeing her for her beauty, she now feels physically and emotionally uncomfortable because the brace is clearly visible to anyone who looks at her. Because of this, she becomes more sympathetic to others who have noticeable health challenges. Deenie even befriends Barbara, a classmate who has eczema, a skin condition that causes rashes.

Deenie also comes to realize that the brace doesn't necessarily change how people feel about her. Buddy, the boy she has a crush on, seems unbothered by it. A classmate, Susan, still admires her and even cuts her own hair to match Deenie's. Her best friends, Midge and Janet, are at first uncomfortable around Deenie and don't know the right thing to say. However, they try to help Deenie get used to the brace, which strengthens their friendship.

Along with coping with the brace, Deenie also wrestles with feelings about her body. She begins to explore her sexuality, and has questions about what's normal. As with *Are You There God? It's Me, Margaret*, some people sought to keep *Deenie* off school library shelves because it contains passages that deal with mature topics.

Following *Deenie*'s publication, Blume continued to tackle teenage challenges. She focused on an especially difficult subject for middle schoolers in her next book, *Blubber* (1974). The novel looks at the bullying of an overweight girl named Linda through the eyes of Jill Brenner, one of her classmates.

One of the striking aspects of *Blubber* is its honest, realistic depiction of bullying. Jill isn't just an innocent bystander in the attacks against Linda—her friend, Wendy, urges her to be a

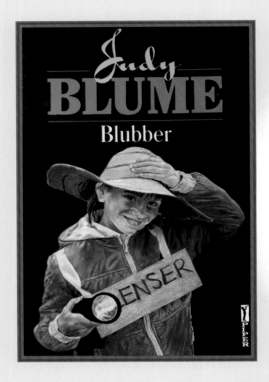

While popular with young readers, *Blubber* was criticized by adults for how it dealt with bullying.

participant in several incidents. Wendy nicknames Linda "Blubber" because of her weight, and is the ringleader in the bullying attacks. Jill goes along with Wendy's schemes largely out of fear.

Blume found some of her inspiration for *Blubber* from her daughter's school experiences. As she wrote in a later edition of the novel, there was a girl much like the character of Wendy in her daughter's fifth grade class. "[This] class leader used her power in an evil way to turn everyone in the class against one girl," wrote Blume.

Jill learns how bullying feels firsthand when Wendy turns against her. Jill challenges Wendy when she uses a racial slur to describe Jill's best friend, Tracy. The next day at school, Jill finds herself the target of Wendy's ire. Wendy even recruits Linda to help out in making Jill miserable. As Wendy's new target, Jill discovers just how vicious her former friend and her allies can be. They give her a nickname, "B. B.," which stands for "Baby Brenner." She is tripped on the bus, attacked at her bus stop, and cornered in the bathroom. By the novel's end, Jill is eventually able to get Wendy and her friends to back off.

Some adults complained about *Blubber* because they were upset that the bullies were never punished for their actions. The lack of consequences, however, rings true for many readers. As Blume herself pointed out in her note in *Blubber*, many students don't report incidents of bullying, and like Jill's teacher, some adults completely miss the signs that a student is being harassed.

BLUME THE TEACHER

While she never became a teacher in a classroom, Blume's books provided a different sort of education to her readers. Young women found the answers to many of their questions about growing up in her stories. A group of women writers paid tribute to her help and guidance in the 2007 essay collection, *Everything I Needed to Know About Being a Girl I Learned from Judy Blume.* Edited by Jennifer O'Connell, the book includes writing by popular authors Meg Cabot, Megan McCafferty, and many others.

Judy Blume's *Forever* is one of her
most controversial books.

Chapter 4
CREATING CONTROVERSY

By 1975, Judy Blume had acquired a reputation for being candid and direct. Her next book, *Forever* (1975), would continue to push the boundaries as her previous books had. *Forever* explores a teenage girl's first serious relationship. High school senior Katherine meets Michael at a party. He is also a high school senior and lives in a nearby town. The pair begin to date, and eventually enter a physical relationship. The novel discusses several mature topics normally ignored in teen literature.

Blume wrote this book for her daughter, Randy. At the time, the books available to teenagers that involved adult relationships followed a similar plot line. Young women that were sexually active usually ended up getting pregnant in these stories. Their pregnancies were treated as some type of punishment for their behavior. As Blume explained to *School Library Journal*, her daughter asked, "'Couldn't there ever be a book about two really nice kids in high school who love each other and they do it and nothing bad happens?' That's how I got the idea for *Forever*."

Michael and Katherine have deep feelings for each other, pledging to stay together forever. Blume, however, shows how young love is not a fairy tale. The couple must deal with the realities of working summer jobs in different states and going to different colleges. At the end of *Forever*, Katherine realizes that first relationships don't always last.

STRUGGLING AGAINST CENSORSHIP

While *Forever*, *Blubber*, and *Deenie* were published in the 1970s, efforts to ban these novels from schools and libraries didn't really pick up steam until the following decade. In an interview with *Instructor* magazine, Blume said, "I felt alone and frightened when my books first came under attack. I felt angry. But for many years now I've felt sad—sad for the kids—because banning a book sends such a negative message."

To this day, Judy Blume remains dedicated to fighting censorship. She explained on the Random House website that it is important to "take a firm stance" against banning books. "If you give in to one person's demand, you will find yourself giving into many peoples' demands, and we will be left with nothing."

Forever was one of the first novels written for a young adult audience that dealt with the mature subjects in a realistic manner. With this book, Blume became one of the pioneers of the young adult genre. Popular with its teen readers, *Forever* stirred up debate among adults. Even before it hit bookstore shelves, the book's publisher was aware that the novel would create controversy. The publisher labeled *Forever* as being for adults, even though Blume intended it for teenagers. Blume explained to *School Library Journal* that her publisher did this "to protect themselves" and to be able to tell "angry parents or teachers" who complained that the book was clearly marked for an older audience. To this day, *Forever* remains a frequently challenged book for its sexual content. A challenged book is one that someone complained about and asked to be taken off the shelves at a school or a library.

Around the time *Forever* was published, Blume was going through some challenges in her own life. She divorced her first husband, John Blume, in 1975. The following year, Blume married her second husband, Thomas A. Kitchens, and soon relocated to New Mexico with her two children to be with him. This new marriage didn't prove to be a happy one, though. Blume and her second husband split up two years later.

While she struggled in her adult life, Blume returned to her youth for her next major work. She considers *Starring Sally J. Freedman as Herself* (1977) to be her most autobiographical novel. It is easy to see why. Set in the 1940s of Blume's childhood, its main character, Sally, shares many of the same qualities and attributes with the young Judy Blume. Like Blume, Sally has a great imagination. She entertains and even soothes herself by making up stories. Both Blume's and Sally's father work as dentists. They each first live in New Jersey and then move to Florida for a time. For Sally and Blume, the trip south is driven by her parents' concern for an older brother's health. Sally, her mother, brother, and grandmother head to Miami Beach, just as Blume's had. And, like Blume's father, Sally's dad stays behind because he needs to work.

Just as in *Iggie's House*, Blume again uses letters in a story to show a character's inner thoughts and feelings. Because Sally misses her father terribly, she writes to him about her experiences in Miami Beach. She also lets her imagination run away with her at times. Sally convinces herself that one of her neighbors, Mr. Zavodsky, is actually Adolf Hitler. In her mind, Hitler, the leader of Nazi Germany, escaped and went into hiding in Florida after the end of World War II. Sally writes Mr. Zavodsky several threatening letters about what she believes is his true identity. In a way, these letters allow her to vent some of her anger about the war's effect on her family.

The events of World War II cast a shadow over many of the characters in the book. Sally thinks often of her cousin, Lila. Both Lila and her mother Rose were living in Europe during the war. They were killed by the Nazis because they were Jewish. The war deeply influenced Blume's childhood as well. As she explained in a note at the end of the novel, "I was just seven years old when World War II ended, but the war had so colored my early life, it was hard to think of anything else."

After Mr. Zavodsky has a heart attack while walking up the stairs in the apartment building, Sally abandons her fantasy about him being Hitler. At the end of the story, Sally is looking forward to going back to New Jersey. She is excited to see her old friends and has begun making plans to throw a party.

A fan favorite, Farley "Fudge" Drexel Hatcher has appeared in several of Blume's novels.

After delving into her own childhood with *Starring Sally J. Freedman as Herself*, Judy was ready to return to the present—and to well-known and well-loved characters. Blume returned to one of her most popular characters with 1980's *Superfudge*. This time around, Peter and Fudge Hatcher have grown up a bit since the last book—Peter is in sixth grade, and Fudge is starting kindergarten. Peter must cope with going to the same school as his troublesome little brother. The pair of them also get ready to become big brothers to the latest addition to the Hatcher family.

Blume later wrote two more Fudge-focused books: *Fudge-A-Mania* (1990) and *Double Fudge* (2002). She created *Double Fudge* after her grandson, Elliot, pestered her for more Fudge stories. The character of Fudge also served as the inspiration for the television show *Fudge*, which aired from 1995 to 1997.

Judy Blume takes questions from fans
at a bookstore in Michigan.

Chapter 5
A WRITER FOR ALL AGES

With her novel *Tiger Eyes* (1981), Blume turned her attention to a teen in crisis. During the summer before she was to start high school, Davey Wexler's father was murdered during a robbery of the convenience store he ran. Overcome with shock and grief, Davey retreats to her room where she chooses to stay in her bed for days on end, not eating.

She is forced to emerge, however, when the school year begins. While her younger brother Jason is excited about going back to school, Davey seems overwhelmed. The combination of a new school and her father's death prove to be too much for her. She passes out a few times at school from panic attacks.

After her doctor recommends she get away for a while, Davey goes with her mother and brother to visit family in New Mexico. Her father's sister, Bitsy, lives there with her husband Walter, a physicist, who works at the Los Alamos National Laboratory.

Davey ends up staying in New Mexico longer than expected when her mother starts suffering terrible headaches. While her

THE LAB OF LOS ALAMOS

Los Alamos, New Mexico is home to the Los Alamos National Laboratory, a famous scientific research center created in 1943. A group of scientists led by J. Robert Oppenheimer worked there. Their mission was to create an atomic bomb. It was thought that such a weapon could help end World War II.

Working with General Leslie R. Groves, Oppenheimer and his team developed the first

This photograph from the 1950s shows a mushroom-shaped cloud caused by an atomic bomb explosion.

atomic bomb in 1945. They tested their new weapon that July in an area south of Los Alamos. The war in Europe was done by this time, but the United States was still battling Japanese forces. Two atomic bombs were used on targets in Japan—the first, nicknamed "Little Boy," was dropped on Hiroshima, and the other, named "Fat Man," was dropped on Nagasaki. After these attacks, Japan finally surrendered, officially ending World War II.

mother retreats from the family, Davey struggles with yet another new school and her overprotective aunt and uncle. One bright spot for Davey is her friendship with a young man named Wolf. The pair meet while Davey explores a local canyon. They later run into each other at the hospital where Davey works as a volunteer. Wolf understands a bit of what Davey is going through, since his own father is dying of cancer.

After Wolf's father dies, he returns to California. Davey writes letters to him about her own father. She also starts to see a therapist to help her work through her grief about her father's violent death. Davey's mother manages to pull herself together, and resumes her place as the head of the family. She decides that it's time for them to return to Atlantic City. While the book ends on a positive note, *Tiger Eyes* remains one of Blume's most challenged works. People have sought to ban this book from schools and libraries for its discussions of violence, alcoholism, and suicide.

By the time *Tiger Eyes* hit bookstore shelves, Blume was going through another series of changes in her personal life. She had separated from her second husband in 1978. Around the time *Tiger Eyes* was published, she started dating George Cooper, a former law professor whom she met in 1980. The pair quickly proved to be inseparable, and were married in 1987.

Blume returned to writing for younger audiences with *The Pain and the Great One* (1984). The story was inspired by Blume's own children when Randy was eight years old and Lawrence was six. Blume's only published picture book, this funny story about sibling

Judy Blume has found happiness with her third husband, George Cooper.

rivalry features a big sister who is referred to as "the Great One" by her little brother. In contrast, she considers her brother to be "the Pain."

In 1987, Blume published her next novel for middle school readers. *Just as Long as We're Together* looks at the friendship between Stephanie, the novel's narrator and main character, and her best friend, Rachel. Their relationship is tested when a new girl named Alison moves into the neighborhood.

Much of the story deals with Stephanie's feelings about her parents' separation. Stressed out by their possible divorce, she turns to food for comfort. By the novel's end, Stephanie eventually gets family and friends to help her cope, instead of turning to food. Through this, Blume once again shows her readers an example of how to handle a difficult, real-life situation.

Blume was so captivated by the characters from *Just as Long as We're Together* that she used Rachel as the focus over her next book. In *Here's to You, Rachel Robinson*, Rachel grapples with acne, a common teenage problem. In an interview, Blume explained to *Entertainment Weekly* that, "My kids both had acne and I never saw a book dealing with the subject."

Just as Long as We're Together deals with friendship and family troubles.

When she's not writing, Judy Blume
likes to spend time outdoors.

Chapter 6
BLUME AT WORK AND PLAY

More than forty years after the publication of her first book, Judy Blume continues to create new stories for her readers. She recently revisited the characters of *The Pain and the Great One* in a series of chapter books, including *Soupy Saturdays with the Pain and the Great One* (2007) and *Friend or Fiend? with the Pain and the Great One* (2009).

Blume has also embraced new ways of communicating with her fans. She started using the social media site Twitter in 2009, and now boasts more than 100,000 followers. "I have a wonderful Twitter universe out there, and we're always talking," she told Neal Conan on the radio program *Talk of the Nation*. "Many people who follow me and whom I follow in return are writers for young people, and I feel this sense of community."

Blume also writes a blog, through which she has shared some of her own personal struggles. In 2012, she was diagnosed with breast cancer. She later underwent surgery and received treatment to battle the disease. On her blog, Blume wrote that she was grateful to those who stood by her through this difficult time, stating,

Judy Blume joins her son, Lawrence, and actress Amy Jo Johnson at the New York premiere of *Tiger Eyes*.

"My friends who've had breast cancer have been so helpful and supportive I can never thank them enough."

Around this time, Blume was working on a special project. She teamed up with her son Lawrence to make one of her stories into a film. The pair brought *Tiger Eyes* to the big screen in June of 2013. "It has always been Larry's favorite," Blume explained to *Publishers Weekly*. "He feels very close to it because he came to live in New Mexico as a young teenager."

In all, Blume and her son spent two years making the movie. It was filmed near Los Alamos, New Mexico, over the course of twenty-three days. Blume stayed on the movie set for the entire time, working alongside her son. In the film, actress Willa Holland plays Davey, and Tatanka Means plays Wolf. Although Davey is a few years older in the screen version than in the novel, the film otherwise remained true to Blume's original story.

In addition to her writing life, Blume is busy with a number of different projects. She serves on the boards of both the Author's Guild and the Society of Children's Book Writers and Illustrators. An ardent opponent of censorship, she has aided the National Coalition Against Censorship over the years. Blume has also established her own educational and charitable foundation, called The KIDS Fund.

Blume enjoys a lot of outdoor activities, and is especially fond of kayaking and biking. A lifelong fan of the movies, she has helped out with creating the Tropic Cinema in Key West, Florida. She and her husband George spend part of their time at their home there. Blume has even worked the ticket booth at this nonprofit movie theater.

Of course, Judy Blume still spends most of her time writing. Each of her books begins with its characters. She writes about

LIKE MOTHER, LIKE DAUGHTER

Judy Blume isn't the only author in her family. Her daughter Randy wrote a novel based on her experiences as an airline pilot for Continental Airlines. *Crazy in the Cockpit: A Woman Pilot's Adventures* was published in 1999. The book follows main character Kendra Davis's journey to becoming a professional pilot, and details the obstacles she encounters along the way.

them in a notebook before she ever sits down to work on the actual plot of the novel. As Blume said in an interview for the Scholastic website, "That way I never feel alone with a blank page or a blank screen." She writes in the morning, spending several hours each day at her desk.

Blume works through at least five drafts of each book. With her first draft, she works on forming all of "the pieces to a jigsaw puzzle" as she explained to the Reading Rockets website. "The second draft is trying to put them together, and then I have to sand them down and make them smooth. Then I paint them wonderful colors, and then I have to polish the whole puzzle so it looks really pretty and finished."

Coming up with titles can be a challenge for Blume. She usually doesn't decide on what to call a book until the very end of the writing process. Sometimes she finds inspiration for her titles inside her own stories. *Then Again, Maybe I Won't* is a phrase that the main character keeps repeating. *As Long As We're Together* comes from a song the three friends sing in the story.

Blume has several suggestions for those who want to follow in her footsteps. For her, great stories mean great characters. She writes on her website that "if you don't care about your characters, your readers won't either." When it comes time to revise a story, she suggests, "Read your work out loud… When you read aloud you find out how much can be cut, how much is unnecessary. You hear how the story flows." She points out that reading aloud is especially helpful when writing dialogue, too.

At book signings, Judy Blume encourages young writers to work hard on their stories.

Dedication and persistence are two other important parts of being a writer. Early in her career, Blume had a few people tell her she couldn't write. She ignored them and kept on working on her stories. She advises other would-be writers to do the same. "Don't let anyone discourage you," Blume said on the Scholastic website. She explains that "no one chooses to become a writer. You write because you can't not write."

Now in her seventies, Judy Blume still can't stop writing. She promises fans that, "I have so many more stories to tell." The little girl who was too shy to write down her stories is now one of the most popular writers in the world, and continues to create characters that kids and adults alike can relate to.

BOOKS BY JUDY BLUME

The One in the Middle Is the Green Kangaroo (1969)

Iggie's House (1970)

Are You There God? It's Me, Margaret (1970)

Then Again, Maybe I Won't (1971)

Freckle Juice (1971)

It's Not the End of the World (1972)

Tales of a Fourth Grade Nothing (1972)

Otherwise Known as Sheila the Great (1972)

Deenie (1973)

Blubber (1974)

Forever (1975)

Starring Sally J. Freedman as Herself (1977)

Superfudge (1980)

Tiger Eyes (1981)

The Pain and the Great One (1984)

Just as Long as We're Together (1987)

Fudge-a-mania (1990)

Here's to You, Rachel Robinson (1993)

Double Fudge (2002)

Soupy Saturdays with the Pain and the Great One (2007)

Cool Zone with the Pain and the Great One (2008)

Going, Going, Gone! with the Pain and the Great One (2008)

Friend or Fiend? with the Pain and the Great One (2009)

GLOSSARY

alcoholism—excessive and out-of-control drinking of alcohol

archenemy—greatest foe or opponent

atomic bomb—a very powerful weapon that creates a huge explosion

autobiographical—writing about one's own life

avid—eager, enthusiastic

censorship—the act of removing or denying access to a book or other work because of its content

eczema—a disease that causes a person's skin to become red, itchy, and flaky

prejudice—an unfair opinion of a person or group of people based on their religion, race, or other factor

scoliosis—a condition in which the spine curves abnormally

technique—a method or way of doing something

CHRONOLOGY

February 12, 1938: Judy Blume is born Judith Sussman in Elizabeth, New Jersey.

1959: Judy marries John M. Blume. Her father dies.

1961: Judy graduates from New York University with a degree in teaching. Daughter Randy Lee is born.

1963: Judy's son Lawrence is born.

1966: Judy takes a writing class at New York University with writer and editor Jane Lee Wyndham.

1969: Judy publishes her first book *The One in the Middle Is the Green Kangaroo*.

1970: Judy publishes *Are You There God? It's Me, Margaret*.

1974: Judy publishes *Blubber*.

1975: Judy divorces her first husband.

1976: Judy marries her second husband, Thomas A. Kitchens, and moves to New Mexico.

1978: Judy divorces her second husband, and publishes her first adult novel *Wifey*.

1983: Judy wins the Eleanor Roosevelt Humanitarian Award.

1987: Judy marries her third husband, George Cooper.

1991: A movie version of *Otherwise Known as Sheila the Great* airs on television.

1995: A TV series based on Judy's Fudge characters begins airing.

2012: Judy battles breast cancer.

2013: Judy and her son Lawrence release the movie version of *Tiger Eyes*.

FURTHER INFORMATION

Books

Jones, Jen. *Judy Blume: Fearless Storyteller for Teens.* Berkeley Heights, NJ: Enslow Publishers Inc., 2008.

Tracy, Kathleen. *Judy Blume: A Biography.* Westport, CT: Greenwood Press, 2007.

Websites

The official Judy Blume website:

judyblume.com/home.php

Visit this site to learn more about Judy's life and books.

Follow Judy Blume on Twitter:

twitter.com/judyblume

Find out the latest on Judy on Twitter.

Visit Judy Blume's fan page on Facebook:

www.facebook.com/ItsMeJudyBlume

Connect with Judy and her fans on Facebook.

BIBLIOGRAPHY

BOOKS

Blume, Judy. *Letters to Judy: What Your Kids Wish They Could Tell You.* New York, NY: G. P. Putnam's Sons, 1986.

Bondoc, Anna and Meg Daly, eds. *Letters of Intent.* Free Press, 1999.

Marcus, Leonard S., ed. *Author Talk.* New York, NY: Simon & Schuster Books for Young Readers, 2000.

Silvey, Anna, ed. *The Essential Guide to Children's Books and Their Creators.* New York, NY: Houghton Mifflin, 2002.

PRINT ARTICLES

Blume, Judy. "Oh, Brother." *Seventeen*, October 2007.

Butnick, Stephanie. "Judy Blume: Still Awesome." *Tablet Magazine*, March 31, 2011.

Corbett, Sue. "Tiger Eyes: A Family Film." *Publishers Weekly*, May 6, 2013.

Freeman, Judy. "Talking with Judy Blume." *Instructor*, May–June 2005.

Solochek, Jeffery S. "Author Blume defends book." *St. Petersburg Times*, January 31, 2004.

Stewart, Susan. "Judy Blume: Q & A." *Entertainment Weekly*, October 29, 1993.

Sutton, Roger. "Forever . . . Yours: An Interview with Judy Blume." *School Library Journal*, June 1996.

ONLINE SOURCES

"Judy Blume." Scholastic website. Retrieved January 6, 2014 from http://www.scholastic.com/teachers/contributor/judy-blume

"Meet the Writers: Judy Blume." Barnes & Noble website. Retrieved January 6, 2014 from http://podbay.fm/show/177873061/e/1190725200

Metz, Nina. "Judy Blume, Forever." *Chicago Tribune* online edition, May 5, 2013. Retrieved January 6, 2014 from http://articles.chicagotribune.com/2013-05-31/features/ct-prj-0602-judy-blume-tiger-eyes-20130531_1_judy-blume-margaret-simon-printers-row-journal

"Most Frequently Challenged Authors of the 21st Century." American Library Association website. Retrieved January 6, 2014 from http://www.ala.org/bbooks/frequentlychallengedbooks/challengedauthors

"Our History." Los Alamos National Laboratory website. Retrieved January 6, 2014 from http://www.lanl.gov/about/history-innovation/index.php

Rosen, Katerina. "Judy Blume on the Death of Her 'Go For It' Father." Huffington Post Live, June 10, 2013. Retrieved January 6, 2014 from http://www.huffingtonpost.com/2013/06/10/judy-blume-father-death_n_3416576.html

"Transcript from an interview with Judy Blume." Reading Rockets website. Retrieved January 6, 2014 from http://www.readingrockets.org/books/interviews/blume/transcript/

INDEX

Page numbers in **boldface** are illustrations.

ABOUT THE AUTHOR:

Wendy Mead spends much of her time writing about other people's lives. She has written several biographies, including *Sharon Creech* for the *Spotlight On Children's Authors* series. Wendy lives in Connecticut with her book-loving family.